Find *HIM*, Now!

By Roger Ernest Billyard, J.D., D.D.

Published by Thistle and Star Ventures
United States of America

Scripture quotations, if included, are used for educational and inspirational purposes.

Paperback ISBN: 979-8-9939755-0-4

Printed in the United States of America.

Contents

Dedicated to my witty, genius, caring, and generous wife,

Margaret "Peg" Ann Eberle Billyard

Prologue

People say, "You're as young as you feel." Well, at 82 years old, I feel young enough to write this book. Living the past 31 years as a recovering addict, I've learned the value and strength of relating one's own experience in an effort to offer hope for recovery from addiction. Thusly, a new way of life becomes available for those seeking recovery. The book at hand expands experience into the realm of observation and belief.

-Roger Ernest Billyard

Chapter 1

Creation

The book, <u>Alcoholics Anonymous</u>, commonly known as <u>The Big Book</u> boldly states, "...there is One who has all power—that One is God." [1] That is a profound statement. Belief in this statement explains an awful lot about humankind's continuing struggle in personal and worldly affairs.

God, exclusively, has all the power. People mistakenly believe that they have power. Actually, they are merely operating under the illusion that they have power. Power is not even a human attribute. [2] Humans are, or at least can be, channels for the power of God. The only way humans can avail themselves of power is by means of God. Surely, therefore, in order to avail oneself of God's power, one needs to believe in the existence of God.

---

[1] "<u>The Big Book</u>", <u>Alcoholics Anonymous</u>, page 59.
[2] <u>Just For Today</u>, Narcotics Anonymous, page 38.

Many come to believe in God as a result of their upbringing. The Bible notes, "Train up a boy according to the way for him; even when he grows old he will not turn aside from it."[3]

Others appear to have a family, social, or religious community that believes in God. They come to share this belief in God that others have. Moses asked God to tell him whom he should tell Israel was the one that had sent him. "God said to Moses, 'I AM WHO I AM'. And he said, 'Say this to the people of Israel, 'I AM has sent me to you.'"[4] This was God's statement of His eternal existence, omnipotence, and unchanging essence.

One need only be open to the possibility that God might exist. Once the possibility of the existence of God is accepted, then one merely needs to be open-minded enough to look at the evidence. It helps to stop calling miracles mere coincidence, and to cease just taking them for granted. Then we can plainly see the evidence.

---

[3] Proverbs 22:6 New World Translation of the Holy Scriptures.
[4] Exodus 3:14 Oxford Annotated Bible, Revised Standard Version.

Truly, the evidence is available for everyone to see. Merely being open to the possibility that God might exist opens the door to looking at this evidence of God's existence.

Look at God's creations. A woman looking out the airplane window, while flying high above the clouds exclaimed, "One can certainly see the handiwork of God." A mother walking along the country lane in the moonless, dark night looking up at the stars with her son was heard to say, "Look at the awesomeness of God's creation."

There is the miracle of gravity. A child spinning a top quickly learns that anything on the top's surface, be it water or some other foreign object, quickly flies off the top's surface as it spins. The Earth, although spinning at more than one thousand miles per hour on its surface at the equator, holds everything on its surface, including oceans of water. Observe a chain of skaters holding hands, and spinning in a circle, moving faster and faster. One notices that the skaters on the outside of the line spin faster than the individuals near the center or axis of the line. The speed and force exerted on the skaters on the outside of the line forces them to let go and spin off on their own. Similarly, the Earth spins slower at its axes, or poles. Still, nothing falls off the Earth's surface, even at its poles. Even at the slowly rotating South Pole nothing falls off the bottom of the earth. Hence, we see miracles as evidence of a Supreme Creator, God.

There is more evidence. The Earth travels around the Sun at an average speed over 65,000 miles per hour, yet it stays in its elliptical orbit with miraculous precision. As if that's not enough, while this is happening, the moon travels around the earth at a speed of more than 2,200 miles per hour. In our own solar system, and countless other solar systems, planets revolve around their suns and moons around their planets with mathematically precise elliptical orbits.[5] WOW! It appears that this All Powerful God uses his creative power to

---

[5] Kepler's equation for elliptical orbits: $a(1-e2)r=1+e\cos\theta$.

perform miracles on Earth and throughout the universe.

For some, seeing evidence of God working in their own lives, as well in the lives of others, is even more compelling evidence of God's existence. Philosopher Frederick Nietzsche was incorrect when he repeatedly stated and advanced the lie, "God is dead."[6] In today's world, there is evidence that God is fully alive, and working many miracles in the lives of humans in recovery programs. Programs of recovery from alcoholism, drug addiction, sex and love addiction, overeating addiction, gambling addiction, and many other addictions rely on trusting in a God of each individual's own understanding. Rather than relying on religion for the doctrines and dogma defining God, these Twelve Step programs allow each individual to reach their own definition and understanding of God. Evidently, this innovative way of approaching God is pure genius. These spiritual, rather than religious, programs allow

---

[6] The Joyous Science by Frederick Nietzsche, and Thus Spoke Zarathustra by Frederick Nietzsche.

individuals to rely on God to help them abstain from their life-threatening addictions. The miracle is that this abstinence was unachievable by themselves, alone. These recovery programs present current, everyday proof that God exists, and works in the lives of those who believe in Him.

It seems very foolish not to be open to seeing all this evidence and proof of the existence of God. "The fool says in his heart, 'There is no God'."[7]

The professed atheist was instructed by a wiser person to create a flower, and return with it for display. That mission has yet to be accomplished.

The guardian angel, Lucifer, who became known as Satan the Devil after his downfall in the Garden of Eden, certainly believes in God.....as do his demons. "Believing in one God? Well, remember that the demons believe this too - so strongly that they tremble in terror." [8]

---

[7] Psalms 14:1 & 53:1 Oxford Annotated Bible, Revised Standard Version.
[8] James 2:19 The Living Bible, Paraphrased.

Chapter 2

Lies

Let's take a closer look at Adam and Eve, the first human couple. Looking back to the beginning of humankind is important for an understanding of our existence, human history, and our place in the world today. The Bible is widely accepted as the written word of God. If God can create the universe and everything therein, God is certainly more than capable of influencing and inspiring humankind to write the Holy Bible. "The whole Bible was given to us by inspiration from God and is useful to teach us what is true and to make us realize what is wrong in our lives: it straightens us out and helps us to do what is right."[9]

God started off the first human couple in the earthly paradise, Garden of Eden. The Garden of Eden was a further manifestation of God's creative power. It was a place of life, love, truth, perfection,

---

[9] 2 Timothy 3:16 The Living Bible, Paraphrased.

goodness, harmony, beauty, peace, and innocence.

Satan, formerly known as Lucifer[10], that fallen angel who oversaw the Garden of Eden, had apparently grown tired of God's love. Inasmuch as misery seeks company, he decided to interject his negative influence and persuasion over the two humans with a lie. God provided many fruit bearing trees in the Garden of Eden, including the tree of life. However, there was one tree in the center of the garden, the tree of good and evil, and they were forbidden from eating its fruit. God had said, "...you must not eat from it, for in the day you eat from it you will positively die".[11] Satan, by means of the serpent, spoke to Eve and contradicted God, "...You will not die. For God knows when you eat of it your eyes will be opened, and you will be like God, knowing good and evil".[12]

Adam and Eve already knew "good". Throughout the creative days, God repeatedly said

---

[10] Isaiah 14:12 King James Version.

[11] Genesis 2:17 New World Translation of the Holy Scriptures.

[12] Genesis 3:4 & 5 Oxford Annotated Bible, Revised Standard Version.

that He saw that it was "good".[13] The first couple was living in the "good" creation. They already knew "good". They most certainly knew God's love and power, and were enjoying the beauty, peacefulness, harmony, and goodness of God's creations. Therefore, it must have been knowing "evil" that would supposedly make them become like God.

Now, man had been created in God's image, according to His likeness.[14] So, humans were already godlike. Therefore, Satan was really referring to something else when he said Adam and Eve would become like God. He was referring to them supposedly having their own individual power, apart from the True God's almighty power. Inasmuch as power is not a human attribute, Satan was once again lying, and, thus, becoming the father of lies.[15]

As far as knowing evil, Satan, himself, was the personification of evil they came to know. The rest

---

[13] Genesis 1:3 - 31 Oxford Annotated Bible, Revised Standard Version.
[14] Genesis 1:26 Oxford Annotated Bible, Revised Standard Version.
[15] John 8:44 Oxford Annotated Bible, Revised Standard Version.

of humankind eventually came to know Satan's influential, persuasive, evil ways, as well.[16] Yes, the results of the sin and disobedience of Adam and Eve spread to all humankind. All came to know Satan's sinful, negative, violent and destructive evil ways. All of which are rooted in the strength of lies.

Adam and Eve turned their backs on God and His love. They chose to disobey his deadly warning about the tree of good and evil. They chose to turn away from God's love, power, goodness, and truth. God's love was insufficient for them. Since "God is love",[17] the conclusion is that God, Himself, was insufficient for them.

Adam and Eve lost their perfection. Now, they would die. Now, they were corrupted. Now, they knew evil. They had lost their innocence. Their character became flawed. They now felt fear, shame, and regret. They felt the weight of their sins: pride, envy, greed, anger, lust, laziness, and

---

[16] 1 John 5:19 Oxford Annotated Bible, Revised Standard Version.
[17] 1 John 4:8 Oxford Annotated Bible, Revised Standard Version.

gluttony. Pride enhanced their god-like feeling with its imitation of power. Such was the closest they would come to fulfilling Satan's lie that they would become like God.

God expelled Adam and Eve from the Garden of Eden without access to the tree of life.[18] Thus, they died. Yes, they died within one day, that is to say within one of God's days. "But do not ignore this one fact, beloved, that with the Lord one day is as a thousand years, and a thousand years as one day."[19] The Bible records in Genesis 5:5, "So all the days of Adam that he lived amounted to nine hundred and thirty years and he died."[20] In fact, no human has lived beyond 1,000 years. As far as anyone knows, the human that lived the longest was Methuselah, who lived to be nine hundred and sixty nine years old.[21]

Humankind through the centuries has been living the lie that they were like God. That is to say,

---

[18] Genesis 2:9 & 3:22-24 Oxford Annotated Bible, Revised Standard Version.
[19] Genesis 3:8 Oxford Annotated Bible, Revised Standard Version.
[20] Genesis 5:5 New World Translation of the Holy Scriptures.
[21] Genesis 5:27 New World Translation of the Holy Scriptures.

humans believed they had god-like power. Even today, humans believe that they have god-like power. Time and time again, they have engaged in warfare, evidently in an attempt to display and show others their god-like power. Humankind now knows evil, and has no hesitation in expressing such. Unfortunately, this god-like power that humans supposedly have is nothing more than the result of being under the influence of the destructive, violent, negative force of Satan.

Satan is solely an influencing force. He has no inherent power of his own. As the Bible puts it, he is merely "prince of the power of the air".[22] However, Satan's influence and mendacious lying must not be underestimated. "And the great dragon was thrown down, that ancient serpent, who is called the Devil and Satan, the deceiver of the whole world - he was thrown down to the earth, and his angels were thrown down with him."[23] Many of Earth's rulers fall under the influence of Satan's deception. Any challenge to the ruler's lies

---

[22] Ephesians 2:2 Oxford Annotated Bible, Revised Standard Version.
[23] Revelation 12:9 Oxford Annotated Bible, Revised Standard Version.

and deceptions are often met with bullying behaviors.   People attempting to point out the truth in the face of the ruler's lies, misrepresentations, exaggerations, half-truths, and sometimes plausible tales, are generally met with insults and intimidation. In addition, tactics of misdirection and diversion are used. When all else fails, threats, violence, destruction, and death may be deemed necessary by the ruler.

Killing one another is the extreme case of Satan's influence. From the beginning, man has killed man. Cain killed his brother, Able. How painful the knowing of evil must have been for Adam and Eve on this occasion. With one of their sons killing his brother, oh, how their grief and regret must have made them yearn for a return to the peace and love that was theirs in the Garden of Eden.

Cain was asked about Able's whereabouts. Cain responded, "I do not know; am I my brother's keeper?"[24] Cain shows by his response that he is

---

[24] Genesis 4:9 Oxford Annotated Bible, Revised Standard Version.

still feeling the influence of Satan, the father of lies. He says he does not know, trying to divert attention away from truthfully answering the question by saying Abel is lying dead in the field. Instead, he asks a manipulative question, trying to direct attention away from further questioning. Cain tries to avoid the ultimate question of how Abel died. Instead of practicing brotherly love, Cain was overwhelmed with envy and anger, thus killing his brother. He became afraid. He wanted to avoid responsibility for his sinful deed.

The illusion of having power manifests itself on a personal level in the everyday lives of all. From time to time, like Adam and Eve, each of us wants to push God to the side, and do things our own way. Our own way, at these particular times, appears to us to be better than God's way. Doing things our own way generally means putting ourselves first. Cane's inquiry as to whether he was his brother's keeper, illustrates the point of desiring to keep oneself first, before and above others. King Solomon in the Bible Book of

Proverbs warns that "All the ways of a man are pure in his own eyes", and again, "Every way of a man is right in his own eyes".[25] Thus, it appears that members of the human race are capable of rationalizing or justifying some pretty outrageous conduct. Always seeking to mislead self and others, or tell the most plausible lie as their defense.

Although written over 2500 years ago, it would be wise for humans to heed Solomon's words, today.   Currently, humans are seemingly in a lightning-speed race to create robots with Artificial Intelligence (AI). On the current trajectory, these robots would be stronger than, and smarter than, humans. It seems that the robots would quickly discern that humans are a threat to the survival of their home planet. Humans generally pay little attention to the effects of global warming, which they like to euphemistically refer to as climate change. Humans generally pay little attention to the effects of environmental and

---

[25] Proverbs 16:2 & 21:2 Oxford Annotated Bible, Revised Standard Version.

ecological balance. Therefore, the robots with their superior artificial intelligence must logically conclude that humans are harmful and unnecessary, and need to be eliminated in order to ensure the planet's survival. The robots will clearly see their need to take over and save the planet. The Artificial Intelligence being developed today, seems to be creating yesterday's science fiction, as tomorrow's reality. Ouch!

From the beginning humans have freely chosen to know evil. Let's not blame God for the free will choices made by humans. Humans have freely chosen warfare, genocide, and the enslavement of other humans.   The evil and self-serving choices of humankind have clearly demonstrated humankind's inability to govern themselves, even in today's world.

In our own time, humanity's rebellion against God, along with their fears, have led them to the capability of destroying themselves with atomic warfare.   Today, more than 12,000 nuclear weapons are distributed among nine nations

(United States, Russia, China, United Kingdom, France, North Korea, India, Pakistan, and Israel). Governments mistakenly believe that peace can be obtained through strength and might. However, the actual result is the increase of fear among humans. Nations seem to categorically reject the notion that peace can be obtained through love and kindness.

There is the pursuit of robots with Artificial Intelligence that may wind up destroying the human race. As if that were not enough, the proliferation of nuclear weapons amongst the nations of the world could also wind up destroying the human race. According to Bible prophecy such a catastrophe will occur, "For then there will be great tribulation, such has not been seen from the beginning of the world until now, no, and never will be. And if those days had not been shortened, no human being would be saved; but for the sake of the elect those days will be shortened."[26]

At that time, when humankind has clearly demonstrated their complete inability to govern

---

[26] Matthew 24:21 & 22, Oxford Annotated Bible, Revised Standard Version.

themselves, and their apparent destiny to totally annihilate themselves, God will intervene. God will intervene, shorten those days of destruction, and prevent humankind from totally killing every single one of themselves. Humankind's power illusion will have been exposed and proven futile. The power Illusion will have been exposed as leading only to violence, destruction, and death.

The power illusion is strong, and, indeed, inescapable in each of us. Our power illusion can manifest itself through our inevitable practice of the so-called seven deadly sins. Alcoholics Anonymous defines these sins, or character defects, as pride, envy, greed, anger, lust, gluttony, and sloth as being universal to all of us.[27] As the Apostle Paul put it, "Therefore, just as sin entered the world through one man, and death through sin, and in this way death came to all people, because all sinned—."[28] Later, the Apostle goes on to explain his own dilemma. "I do not

---

[27] Twelve Steps and Twelve Traditions, Alcoholics Anonymous, page 64.
[28] Romans 5:12 New International Version.

understand my own actions. For I do not do what I want, but I do the very thing I hate."[29]

Fear plays a large part in all of this. When we deny God's existence, or push God aside, we are left to our own devices, our own way of thinking. We become self-centered. Ego, rebellion, negativity, and self-obsessive fear then drives us to feeling these seven deadly sins, which are essentially defects in our corrupted character. These feelings drive our submission to expressing ourselves and behaving in accord with sins and character defects. Feeling these defects of character can lead us to undesirable, sinful behavior. Negativity, shortcomings, dishonesty, violence, and destruction become our deadly ways. All the result of turning our backs on God.

Pride appears to be the keystone of sins and character defects. Pride urges us to edge God

---

[29] Romans 7;15 Oxford Annotated Bible, Revised Standard Version.

out and do things our own way. It leads us into denying God's love, and substituting our own will for God's will. Pride allows us to see ourselves above others, and enables us to justify our self serving conduct.

Once entrenched in pride, we can easily move on to envy, to admire and seek that which may likely be to our detriment.

Greed will easily lead to garnering and hoarding things to ourselves, at the expense of sharing love and achievements with others.

Anger is easily justified by pride, as we say to ourselves, "How can these things possibly happen to the almighty me."

Pride also justifies lust, as we tell ourselves, "My superiority entitles me to seek whatever or whoever my lust sees as a target." Hence, lust's pursuit proceeds.

Pride always insidiously tells us, "I can eat any quantity I want of whatever I want, and suffer no health consequences whatsoever." Pride is quick to assure that we can handle it all.

Pride permits any sloth I might be feeling. My arrogant attitude says, "I don't have to do this", or "I don't have to do that", and in particular, "I don't have to do anything, today."

When Adam and Eve committed the original sin by eating that forbidden fruit, and thus turning away from God, they became fearful and hid.[30] As the Apostle Paul pointed out, sin has spread to all of us, thus creating an internal conflict of doing things God's way or one's own way. There is that ever-present human desire to take control of situations and other people. Fear is the force that pushes one toward doing things one's own way, the sinful way, rebelling and edging God out. One might tell oneself, "I'm afraid I won't get enough to eat or sleep; I'm fearful that I won't get the things I want or need; I'm angry that things did not go my

---

[30] Genesis 3:10 Oxford Annotated Bible, Revised Standard Version.

way, and I fear the catastrophes that might follow."

Adam and Eve willfully chose to rely on Satan's lies. Thus their reality changed. They lost their perfection, paradise, and everlasting life. However, God's truth remained unchanged. Lies always attempt to change reality and avoid responsibility. Nevertheless, truth remains the same. Adam and Eve did indeed die, as has all humanity along with them. As opposed to living in Paradise, they now lived in a world of thorns and thistles.[31]

A boy, in the early morning sunlight, longs for a doughnut from the box he sees on top of the refrigerator. His parents had instructed him, when the doughnuts arrived the previous day, to wait until everyone gets up the next morning to all share in eating the doughnuts. Although only five years old, the boy rebels. He pushes a chair up

---

[31] Genesis 3:18 Oxford Annotated Bible, Revised Standard Version.

against the counter next to the refrigerator. He climbs onto the chair, then onto the counter, and reaches for the box of doughnuts. The boy begins to eat the doughnut of his choice.

Out of the corner of his eye he catches sight of the metal buckle of his father's dreaded army belt laying on the other side of the doughnut box. The belt is wide, thick, and heavy. Fear sweeps over him. His heart drops in his chest. Panic grips him as he contemplates the outcome of his behavior. He knows he should not be eating that doughnut. He remembers all too well previously being spanked with this army belt for eating a doughnut without permission. Presently, the doughnuts had been placed seemingly out of his reach, but only now does he see the menacing belt. Fear clings to the boy, "What can I do to avoid a spanking with this army belt?" His manipulative thinking leads him to rearranging the doughnuts in the box, hoping that eleven doughnuts will now appear to be a full dozen of twelve.

The boy's fear and ego created rebellion, and then came manipulation, which is a close cousin of lying. At the early age of five, the boy is able to experience evil and sin. He behaves in accord with his character defects of greed and perhaps gluttony.

Later that year, the boy is informed that the family is moving to a new house. The boy wants things his way. He wants to stay in the house where he already lives. He is unimpressed by talk about a lovely creek that runs behind the new house. He does not want to move into a new house. Nevertheless, boxes are moved into his current house for packing. The young lad sees a very large box, taller than himself, has been placed in the living room. The boy gets a running start from the kitchen, and delivers a high flying kick to the box. A hole slightly bigger than the size of his foot now appears in the side of the box. Fear, again, overwhelms the boy. He immediately has visions of being spanked with the army belt when his actions are discovered. He has already learned the evilness that lies can change reality, or at least the perception of reality. So, he turns the box so that the hole now faces the wall, in a feeble attempt to cover up his wrongdoing. Later, his parents do discover the hole. He lies to his parents, firmly stating that he did not kick the hole in the box, and that he knows nothing about it. Yes, the boy has again sinned. He has not trusted God would take care of him, even in a new house. He has acted upon his character defects, his feelings of pride and anger.

Adam and Eve did not trust God. They chose not to believe in God's truth. They chose to believe the lie that eating from the tree of good and evil would not kill them. They believed Satan's lie that they would not die. Choosing to act upon Satan's lying led to a change in reality in a huge way. Adam and Eve were cast out of the Garden of Eden as a result. However, God's truth still remained the same.

Lies can change reality, or at the very least one's perception of reality. Certainly, lies are intended to change reality. Whether lies are believed or just tolerated, reality changes. Truth generally brings consequences. Lies are an attempt to avoid accountability and responsibility. Those who tell lies, or just go along with lies, normally feel a change of reality within themselves, as well. Unless an individual doesn't care whether they are discovered in their lying, or just simply have no regard for others, they now feel shame, guilt, and damage to their self-esteem. The shame and guilt snowballs into a loss of freedom within oneself. Those who are associated with lies become imprisoned within themselves by trying to keep track of what was lied about, and to whom which lies were told. The lying has now led to a complex entanglement of different lies being told to different people. Liars, and those who endorse or go along with lies, live in fear of discovery. Personal freedom is lost. They are figuratively hiding out, similar to the way Adam and Eve were literally hiding out after acting upon Satan's lies.[32]

Adam and Eve's new reality was a harsh one. Now, they would grow old and die. Their access to the tree of life, of everlasting life, was now out of their reach.[33]   They would now experience pain and hardship. They would now have to rely on their own imitation of power. Rebellion, ego, and fear would now govern their lives. Satan would now have a greater advantage in tempting them to practice sin, through influencing their corrupted character. Humans were now more vulnerable because of Adam and Eve, and because of their decision to turn away from God's love and power. Humans were no longer perfect, nor were they living in the perfect Garden of Eden with access to

---

[32] Genesis 3:8 Oxford Annotated Bible, Revised Standard Version.
[33] Genesis 3:22-24 Oxford Annotated Bible, Revised Standard Version.

the tree of life. Satan's influence and persuasion would grow to be even stronger. Satan had become "the god of this world", and humankind would pay the price.[34]

Satan is also in trouble. For God stated a prophecy to Satan:

> "And I will put enmity between you and the woman, and between your offspring and hers; he will crush your head, and you will strike his heel." [35]

A "crush" in the head sounds like a death sentence for Satan. Understandably, Satan is angry, "Be alert and of sober mind. Your enemy the devil prowls around like a roaring lion, looking for someone to devour."[36]

---

[34] 2 Corinthians 4:4 Oxford Annotated Bible, Revised Standard Version.
[35] Genesis 3:15 New International Version.
[36] 1 Peter 5:8 Oxford Annotated Bible, Revised Standard Version.

Chapter 3
The Results

Adam and Eve's actions resulted in their corruption. They were no longer perfect. They had lost their innocence. They were now experiencing fear because of turning their backs on God's love, power, instruction, and warning. They turned their back on the everlasting gift of the tree of life. Humans have not obtained the gift of everlasting life on their own, nor has such a gift been obtained from Satan. Clearly humans have no such everlasting life-giving power.

The playwright William Shakespeare describes individuals as "....a poor player, That struts and frets his hour upon the stage, And then is heard no more".[37] Humans suffer a

---

[37] Macbeth, by William Shakespeare, Act V, Scene V.

profound fear and loss that brings forth feelings of emptiness inside. An emptiness which humans continually strive to fill by relying on the exercise of their sinful character defects.

Since being cast out of the Garden of Eden, humans have futilely continued their efforts to fill the feelings of emptiness inside with things outside of themselves. Some of the usual sought after comforts include money, food, sex, violence, the controlling of people, or the controlling of desired outcomes. Any satisfaction achieved is only temporary. The discontent and emptiness promptly returns and continues.

So, it seems that humans have generally been living their lives in various states of dissatisfaction. Such is the result of edging God out, and giving in to one's own ego. The individual is left to cope with feelings of fear, negativity, and rebellion. These feelings serve as an umbrella enveloping a reliance upon sinning; the habit of relying on feelings of pride, envy, greed, anger, lust, gluttony, and laziness; and living life with the practices and behaviors that result. All the while, Satan's temptation and influence encourages us to rely on these sinful behaviors.

Satan begins to establish his influence upon humans from an early age. Satan's destructive and violent influence is seen in cartoons, where violence happening to another appears laughable. Computer games frequently offer the reward of victory, as a result of the violent destruction of something or someone.

Satan's destructive and violent nature also is evidenced in toys. There are toy guns and toy soldiers. There is toy military equipment, such as, aircraft, warships, tanks, battleships, and spaceships. Later in youth, these military, violent, and destructive themes are carried through as entertainment in war movies, crime movies, and horror movies. As adults, many relish violent sports, such as, football, hockey, boxing, and wrestling. Such things help continue and reinforce the illusion that humans have power. However, violence and destruction are not actually power.

Apparently, violence and destruction are the best that Satan has to offer as a substitute for true power. So it is that Satan glorifies all things akin to violence, destruction, and warfare. Trophies are awarded to the victors in sports. Medals are awarded to the best killers in warfare. Satan offers only death, not life. Look back at the huge spectator arenas that have been built for exhibitions of death, whether by gladiators or bullfighters. Oh look, Rome's mighty Coliseum is decaying and crumbling away. Let us rebuild it!

Mark Twain in <u>A Horse's Tale</u> writes about a bull-fight, "....my uncle, the priest, took me as a reward for being a good boy...." and later, "Is the bull-fight a religious service? I think so. I have heard so. It is held on Sunday."[38]   If hoards of people were not attending such spectator arenas for the religious experience, they were certainly going for the entertainment of witnessing violence, destruction, and death. Satan, the roaring lion, devours people with impalements, crucifixions, lynchings, assassinations, executions, murders, and wars.

At age 12 the boy, along with his friend Chuck, were hiking and meandering along the creekside footpath. They came to a clearing, that had more or less, been their destination. The two immediately noticed that a frog had been impaled between two small stakes. The frog was in a spread eagle position, with its four

[38] <u>A Horse's Tale</u>, by Mark Twain, page 83 & 89.

legs bound by strings attaching it to the two steaks. The poor creature's pain and suffering had ended. It was dead. The boy felt immediate repulsion that made him feel sick to his stomach. The boy was deeply saddened. "Who had done this?", he agonized. He immediately knew, without any doubt, that it had been the boys from the neighborhood. His neighborhood had no shortage of bullies. That was for sure. He knew from experience that these bullies enjoyed inflicting pain and suffering. However, this bullying behavior was more than inflicting pain and suffering for enjoyment. Causing this frog's torturous, horrifying death was knowing pure evil. Satan smiled.

The roaring lion had devoured this band of boys. Doubtless, they would move on as adults to become wife beaters, children beaters, rapists, even murderers. Perhaps they would become idolizers and imitators of the soldiers that tortured and killed Jesus in front of his agonizing mother, Mary.

In this particular town, bullying was a practice primarily engaged in by males. Certainly females are entirely capable of engaging in bullying behaviors. Often females support anyone who habitually engages in these behaviors. Many people, regardless of age, race, or sexual identity, support all forms of bullying behaviors.

Satan seems to have established a strong influence on bullies and their behaviors. Bullies have the twisted idea that putting other people down, belittling them, mocking them, physically beating on them, and even killing them will somehow build themselves up, make them feel better about themselves, allow them to feel superior to others, and make them feel more god-like. Bullies have little regard for others. They apparently enjoy seeking their goal of feeling superior and more god-like. Bullies are generally consumed by pride in themselves and their own perceived strength. The bully likes his victims to fear him. At the same time, the bully wants certain others to like him, even to join in with him.   Others do join in with the bully due to their underlying insecurities and low self esteem. They fear that, otherwise, the bully might turn on them.

Bullies like to display bravado, and often amplify it with their use of foul and profane language. They often use vulgar and profane language to put-down and degrade others in an attempt to show superiority and toughness.

When the bully makes fun of another person, he wants followers to laugh along with him. When the bully lies about someone he wants his followers to believe him, or at least go along with him.   Some will go along just because they see others following along. These followers who go along with the bully's profane, violent, and destructive attitudes and behaviors will often imitate them. They too use vulgar language and profanity in seeking an ego inflating feeling of being better-than others, that god-like feeling of having false power. The feeling that comes with having control over other people. The feeling of superiority and pride.

Bullying can also take more subtle forms, such as, joke telling, trickery, criticism, sarcasm, verbal put-downs, wise-cracks, insults, bragging, and mocking. Whenever a person is placed on the receiving end of these sometimes seemingly innocent behaviors they are being bullied to some extent. They are being denigrated so that the bully can feel more knowledgeable, more experienced, wiser, smarter, superior - indeed, more god-like.

The boy, now 13 years old, was in a junior high school shop class, a class which the school had gloriously named Industrial Arts. The boy had grown into being a tall, thin, shall we say lanky fellow. He was often the target of bullying. On this particular day, George, a fellow student, was sweeping the floor with a push broom. George continued to deliberately slam his broom into the boy's feet. The boy repeatedly pleaded with George to stop. Finally, the boy had had enough. His anger gave way to satanic violence, and he gave his most powerful roundhouse punch to the bully's mouth. George's tooth suffered a large chip, and went bouncing across a stack of sheet metal. The entire class had been watching the lead-up to the punch. They were all able to follow the tooth chip as it went "ding, ding, ding", across the stack of sheet metal. George made no response. The boy rightly assumed that bullies are motivated by their own fears. George did not dare retaliate against the boy. George was fearful.

Years later, the boy who was now in college, stopped by a local bar to have a beer. Who should walk in but George. George sat down next to the now much older boy.   Although the boy was now a young man, the two recognized each other immediately. The two spoke, and the boy learned that George lived right across the street. Although George would occasionally edge a little bit closer to the boy, he made no other aggressive movements.   Doubtless the boy's presence reminded George of his underlying fears and insecurities. At such close range, the boy was able to observe that the chip gap remained in George's front tooth.   He surmised that George's fear was still alive and well. Perhaps George's mirror gave him a daily reminder of past events. All the same, the boy decided not to return to that particular bar in the future.

The boy, now thirty years old, visited a mentally-challenged, teenage friend in the hospital. After the two chatted for a while, they decided to play a card game. When the thirty year old said he would get a pen and paper in order to keep score, his teenage friend responded, "no, let's just play". What a novelty! Unnecessary to be a winner. Unnecessary to put somebody down or ridicule them. Unnecessary to prove superiority over the other person. Instead, let our primary focus be on socializing. Let's just be friends.

At age 45, the boy observed an incident that occurred at a Special Olympics event. The race was in progress, when one of the participants stumbled and fell. A runner by his side immediately stopped, and assisted the fallen runner to his feet. Assisting his fellow man was of greater importance than winning the race. He felt no need to prove himself better than the fallen runner, nor better than the others. Winning the race, or proving superiority, was of absolutely no importance when confronted with being able to assist a fellow, fallen human.

The boy, as a 60 year old grandfather, was witness to another incident that occurred when he took his mentally-challenged grandson to the park for a concert event. While waiting for the concert to begin, the grandson noticed a couple of other boys playing in the adjacent playground. He immediately went to the playground to join in activities with his fellows.   When the grandfather looked over toward the playground, he noticed that two other boys were beating on his grandson with plastic swords. The grandfather immediately rushed over to assist his grandson, and admonished the other boys. The grandfather decided they would forgo the concert, and just return home. While walking to the car, the grandfather stopped when he noticed his grandson crying. "What's the matter? Are you hurt?" "No!", the grandson replied, "I just want to go back and play."

These last three incidents seem to prove the adage that folks with special needs are "a little closer to the angels". They appear to naturally have an acceptance and caring for others that many of us struggle to find.   It seems that most of us ordinary people would rather call an individual a bully, instead of solely referring to the bully's behavior. Likewise, most tend to call a person a liar, instead of just saying that the person lies a lot. Instead of judging people, we need to recognize that we have in fact engaged in the same behavior as the person we are condemning, or at the very least are capable of engaging in that same behavior. "'Unconditional love' is not the same as 'unconditional acceptance.' I don't have to like your behavior but that doesn't mean we reject each other as human beings."[39] Let's be continually mindful of that often quoted phrase, "Judge not, that ye be not judged."[40]

At times, an individual uses joke telling to divert another's attention away from engaging in bullying behaviors. Such clever action has oftentimes proven to be successful in escaping from another's violent or destructive behaviors.

However, there are dangers in being a joke teller. In the extreme, the joke teller can use his talent to pursue praise and adulation. He relishes hearing the comment, "Oh, he's so clever!" Joke telling, at times, puts entire groups of people on the negative, receiving end. There are ethnic jokes, dumb blonde jokes, lawyer jokes, and so on.

---

[39] Guiding Principles, Narcotics Anonymous, page 11.
[40] Matthew 7:1 King James Version.

Upon losing a game the individual is often portrayed as being "beaten" or "crushed" or "destroyed". The winner wants to bask in the sunlight of victory; wants to make known his established position of being better than "those losers". These are insidious ways of bullying.

In the extreme case of warfare, the enemy is always referred to by dehumanizing names, such as, rats, vermin, towel-heads, animals, gooks, scum, or krauts. So it is that military leaders, and sometimes rulers, attempt to socialize and entrench particular lies. They wish to perpetuate the lies that some people are lesser than others. Which brings to mind racism and slavery as being other forms of bullying in the extreme. Instead of denigrating one single person, racism and slavery denigrate entire populations. Huge numbers of people eagerly join in. All of them claiming to be better than "those others". All these behaviors reinforce the lie that, "I'm god-like", or certainly that, "I'm more god-like than you".

The evidence of Satan's influence with destruction and violence has continued throughout human history. The record of human history relates the seemingly endless stream of engagement in the destruction and violence of warfare. For a variety of rationales, one nation endeavors to establish dominance over another nation, or in the case of world wars, one group of nations endeavors to establish dominance over another group of nations. Individuals and nations alike use the threat or administration of violence and destruction in an effort to enforce their will. However, this is a poor imitation of true power. Such actions lack creativity and constructive direction.

The strength of Satan's lies, the strength of any and all lies, must not be underestimated. The resulting pain, suffering, and confusion is unavoidable. Just as Satan begins establishing his rebellious, violent, and destructive influence upon humans when they are at a very young age, similarly, he seeks to make lying more attractive by promoting the innocence of the "little white lie". Satan enjoys hearing that someone is telling a little white lie in order to protect another person's feelings. Satan certainly doesn't want someone protecting another person's feelings with tact and love instead of telling them a lie. Telling the little white lie has demonstrated to the person how easy and seemingly beneficial that lying can be. Soon, the person is using lying to duck and dodge the truth. The person says to themself, "Let me see what I can get away with". In particular, the person wants to avoid the consequences that telling the truth can bring upon others or oneself. Thus, little white lies give Satan his desired foothold into leading the person into telling progressively bigger lies in the future.

Many, if not most, games promote lying, deception, and manipulation. Such can be particularly noted in card games, such as, poker, bridge, hearts and spades. Players bluff, make misleading bids, and feign weakness with a strong hand.

Likewise, sports promote deception and manipulation. In baseball, the runners can steal bases. In football, teams routinely use fake and deceptive plays in order to advance the ball and score points.

The young property owner put up a sign stating that his premises are protected by a burglar alarm system, which they were not. Indeed, the young person's premises was not burglarized. The small manufacturing company put up a sign by its dumpster, stating that the premises are protected security cameras, which they were not. Yes, other people stopped throwing their garbage into the company's dumpster. These seemingly innocent, lying gestures can lead those who practice them into delving further into the practice of lying. Satan welcomes all lying, big and small, after all, he is the father of lies. Therefore, we need to live honestly. We need to remember the Apostle John's assurance that "the truth will make you free".[41]

Satan has no power, therefore, he relies upon lies in an attempt to maintain influence and control over humans. His lies have proven to be persuasive and effective. Many fall prey to believing his lies, or at least going along with his lies. Now, these ones are vulnerable. Satan, as a roaring lion, seeks these people out. He observes those who like feeling superior to others and enjoy bullying. He sees their bullying

[41] John 8:32 Oxford Annotated Bible, Revised Standard Version.

behaviors covering up their own fears and cowardliness. He devours them by placing them in leadership roles, where they carry out his evil desires of inflicting torture, suffering, and death upon many others. Satan relishes seeing a ruler's victims being abused, like that distressed, tormented, executed frog.

Satan can also devour people with fear. Fear is contrary to love. Fear favors negativity. Fear can become all consuming in one's life. The Devil uses fear as a breeding ground for arguments, grudges, resentments, retaliation, and revenge. These things lead to hate, violence, destruction, warfare, and death. It can be difficult to find God amongst all the existing chaos and confusion in the world, mostly created by Satan's influence on humankind's sinful tendencies.

Chapter 4

The Solution

The solution requires acceptance. We must accept reality as it is. We cannot successfully lie or pretend reality away. Similarly, we must shun Satan's lies, and stop living in denial of who we truly are. We need to be honest with ourselves and others.

Any of our attempts at bargaining with God do not provide any real solution to today's dilemmas. We must accept the fact that we cannot bargain with God. To say to God, "if you just give me that", or, "if you just do this for me", I will serve you, does not cut the mustard. Remember, it is impossible to bargain with God, because God has all the power. We have no power, hence no bargaining position. In any event, humankind does not have a better solution than God. That being said, sometimes God will give us what we want and what we try to bargain for, and we turn away from Him, anyway.

We need to stop blaming God for the world's situations. We need to stop saying: "Why does God allow this?", "Why did God allow that?", "Why doesn't God stop this?" "How can God allow all this killing?", "Why does God tolerate wars, when he has the power to stop them?" Remember, these situations came about due to the choice of humans, starting with Adam and Eve and their choice to know evil. In essence, humans choose to say, "We do not need Your love or help God. We can handle situations by ourselves."

Although our living situation in this world may seem hopeless, the True God has provided us with a solution.   The solution is provided even though the evil god of this world, Satan the

Devil, is a destructive and violent force always seeking to devour someone. Our choice today is much the same as the choice faced by Adam and Eve. Do we choose to align ourselves with the power of a loving, creative, truthful God? Or, do we choose to align ourselves with the evil, hateful, destructive, violent force of Satan? Do we choose to find and follow God, or do we choose to join with Satan who has turned away from God? Perhaps we have an advantage over Adam and Eve because humankind now knows evil. Thus, today, the choice for us is extremely clear.

Accepting the evidence of the world situation resulting from Satan's lies and the proliferation of lies, makes God's truthful and loving way the obvious choice. Satan's way represents lies and death. God's way represents truth and life.

Truly, the choice is a personal one. It does not necessarily involve the doctrine or dogma of religion which for some creates contradiction and rebellion within oneself. A person can choose to live a spiritual life apart from what some see as the forced guidance and seeming hypocrisy of religion. One can avail themself of a personal relationship with God, and become a channel for His loving, caring power.

Nevertheless, thousands upon thousands of people choose the ways of Satan over the ways of God. Humankind finds it all too easy to choose destruction, violence, and killing. It seems that world leaders need only give permission and instruction to engage in destruction, violence and killing in order for thousands of people to obey. Then when confronted with their shameful actions, these folks attempt to avoid any and all responsibility by giving the usual response, "I was just following orders". We must not allow Satan's temptation and influence over others to make our choice for us.

It may seem like we are living in the worst of times. However, we might, in fact, be living in the best of times. There is, indeed, a great need to turn away from lying and denying reality. We need to seek and find God. God is in essence Love. We do find God to be loving and caring. His caring helps us heal from the certain harm and chaos resulting from lies. God's caring helps us heal from shame, guilt, fear and negativity. We will stop theorizing about spirituality and begin living in spiritual reality. We will begin to realize we are not merely physical creatures trying to live a spiritual life. Rather, we come to know our true nature is spiritual. Then we understand that we are spiritual entities endeavoring to live a physical life. "Do you not know that your body is a temple for the Holy Spirit within you, which you have from God?"[42] We experience a spiritual connection with God, which allows us to serve as channels for His love, truth, guidance, and power.

Making the choice according to who we are, according to our true nature, the choice becomes intuitive. Remembering that we are created in God's image and likeness, finding and choosing God is making our choice in harmony with His universal intent. Looking at the big picture, the universe as a whole, God created mankind "only a little lower than angels".[43] Jesus makes note that humans are children of God. He states, 'Pray then like this: Our Father who art in heaven ....."[44]

Pope Francis addressed humankind's place when speaking to a Muslim congregation. Pope Francis traveled to the central mosque in Bangui, in the Central African Republic, in the heart of the

---

[42] 1 Corinthians 6:19 Oxford Annotated Bible, Revised Standard Version.
[43] Psalms 8:5 The Living Bible, Paraphrase.
[44] Matthew 6:9 Oxford Annotated Bible, Revised Standard Version.

city's Muslim enclave, which has been a flashpoint for violence in recent years where Christians and Muslims killed one another. Pope Francis pointed out the equality existing amongst humans, that they actually are sons and daughters of God, and hence are brothers and sisters. Pope Francis said, "You are sons and daughters of God, just as we are. When all of us begin to get that understanding, don't you think we'll begin to be on a path to peace in our world?"[45]

Even given the introduction of evil into the world, and humankind's sinful and often war-like state, God provided a wonderful opportunity for all humans. "For God so loved the world that he gave his only son, that whoever believes in him should not perish but have eternal life. For God sent the Son into the world, not to condemn the world, but that the world be saved through

---

[45] National Catholic Reporter, January 7, 2016, by Thomas Gumbleton.

him."[46] Jesus, the Son of God, confirmed that he is "the way, the truth, and the life".[47] A tremendous demonstration of God's love for humans. We are reminded that God is Love. Accordingly, we need to choose and behave in harmony with that love.

Whilst some seemingly improve their lives by lying, or even becoming rulers by lying, we must remember who is the "father of lies", and that the ways of lying are the ways of certain death. Finding God, on the other hand, and choosing God's way, provides us with love, truth, and life.

To receive this gift of eternal life, we merely need to believe. "For by grace you have been saved through faith; and this is not your own doing, it is the gift of God - not because of works, lest any man should boast."[48]

---

[46] John 3:16 &17 Oxford Annotated Bible, Revised Standard Version.
[47] John 14:6 Oxford Annotated Bible, Revised Standard Version.
[48] Ephesians 2:8 & 9 Oxford Annotated Bible, Revised Standard Version.

When finding God and making our choice for God over Satan, be reminded of the two commandments given by Jesus. They are commandments of love. We need to love God, and to love our neighbor.[49]   We are choosing to return to God's love - that love which was dismissed by Adam and Eve. As the Dalai Lama XIV puts it, "My religion is kindness".[50] As the Golden Rule stated by the Apostle Luke says, "And as you wish that men would do to you, do so to them".[51] Jesus pushes the envelope even further when in his Sermon on the Mount he says to "love your enemies".[52]

Jesus practiced what he preached.   He displayed love for his enemies as he was being put to death. "And Jesus said, 'Father forgive them; for they know not what they do'."[53]

---

[49] Mark 12:30 & 31 Oxford Annotated Bible, Revised Standard Version.
[50] My Religion Is Kindness, The core of all spiritual and humanistic paths, Tara Brock Bach, PhD.
[51] Luke 6:31 Oxford Annotated Bible, Revised Standard Version.
[52] Matthew 5:44 Oxford Annotated Bible, Revised Standard Version.
[53] Luke 23:34 Oxford Annotated Bible, Revised Standard Version.

Regardless of how grave, shameful or deadly our sins and behaviors are, we must not use them as an excuse to deny God or conclude that we are undeserving saying that, "I am so bad that God doesn't care about me." We must accept God's magnanimous forgiveness and move ahead through any guilt, shame or self-pity that we may feel. Then we can happily and prayerfully accept His will, grace, and guidance on an ongoing basis.

Finding and choosing God is choosing a life of love, happiness, honesty, freedom, joy, and peace. As Jesus said, "For the Kingdom of God is within you."[54]

To find and choose God, is to find and choose love. Remember that we are in God's image and likeness, and remember that God is Love. Although it may sound difficult, we are certainly very capable of love. That love will

---

[54] Luke 17:21 The Living Bible, Paraphrased.

help overcome our fears, and the influence of that violent and destructive force that is seeking to consume us. "Enter by the narrow gate; for the gate is wide and the way is easy, that leads to destruction, and those enter by it are many."[55] In finding God we turn away from our internal urges of sin and lies. Instead, we learn to love ourselves, love others, and love God. There, within ourselves, is found the true freedom given by God. There, within ourselves, we find the Kingdom of God.

Elon Musk bragged about throwing USAID (United States Agency for Internal Development) into the "wood chipper". His actions of virtually destroying USAID stopped United States aid from arriving in poor countries around the world. Bill Gates, cofounder of Microsoft, rightfully pointed out to the Financial Times that "The picture of the world's richest man killing the

---

[55] Matthew 7:13 Oxford Annotated Bible, Revised Standard Version.

world's poorest children is not a pretty one". Jesus' comment comes to mind that, "It is easier for a camel to go through the eye of a needle than for a rich man to enter the kingdom of God".[56]

In the event that one needs further admonishment, "the love of money is the root of all evils".[57] "Throw away your money! Toss it out like worthless rubbish, for it will have no value in that day of wrath. It will neither satisfy nor feed you, for your love of money is the reason for your sin."[58] Also, "Stop storing up for yourselves treasures upon the earth, where moth and rust consume, and where thieves break in and steal."[59] The luxurious living that is afforded by wealth can be very alluring. However, this is no guarantee of true happiness.

---

[56] Mark 10:25 Oxford Annotated Bible, Revised Standard Version.
[57] 1 Timothy 6:10 Oxford Annotated Bible, Revised Standard Version.
[58] Ezekiel 7:19 The Living Bible, Paraphrased.
[59] Matthew 6:19 New World Translation of the Holy Scriptures.

Instead, it can distract one from finding God. Such distraction from God can lead to pain. "By reaching out for this love [of money] some have been led astray from the faith and have stabbed themselves all over with many pains".[60] The Apostle Matthew states, "Rather, store up for yourselves treasures in heaven, where neither moth nor rust consumed, and where thieves do not break in and steal. For where your treasure is there your heart will be also."[61]

Living the wealthy lifestyle has an insidious way of edging God out of the picture. One can develop an attitude of "I have it all". The wealthy person's entire focus can become maintaining and expanding his or her wealth, at the expense of losing any and all contact with God. One easily becomes prone to relying on one's wealth, rather than relying upon God. Yet, if all the wealth, luxury, money, and pretensions are

---

[60] 1 Timothy 6:10 New World Translation of the Holy Scriptures.
[61] Matthew 6:20 & 21 New World Translation of the Holy Scriptures.

stripped away and gone, the rich person is, in essence, exactly the same as the poor person.

Jesus Christ was also confronted with making the choice between God and Satan. Satan tried to influence Jesus, and tempt him by showing Jesus all the kingdoms of the world. Satan would reward Jesus with all of the authority and glory of these kingdoms if Jesus would worship him. Jesus responded that he would only worship and serve God.[62]

Even though the possibility of evil choices abound in the world, God can still be found. His love and power is ever available to us. The existence and effects of evil will cause us pain. However, finding and relying on God will help us to relieve our suffering. God does not forsake those who share in His love and choose to do His will.

---

[62] Luke 4:5-8 Oxford Annotated Bible, Revised Standard Version.

Let's make the same wise choice that Jesus made. Let us choose God's truth instead of Satan's lies. Let us find God in all of His creations on planet Earth, and throughout the entire universe. Most importantly, let us find God within ourselves, within our own hearts. Let's avail ourselves of God's ever present love, and find that Kingdom of God within ourselves.

Yes, the boy grew up to find and choose a loving and caring God. He found God, and the Kingdom of God within himself, primarily by befriending and learning from people who practiced an unconditional love for others.

Remember, God is especially fond of you![63]

---

[63] <u>The Shack</u>, by Wm. Paul Young, page Page 244.

Acknowledgements

Many thanks to my three wonderful children, Kimberly O. Billyard, Gael J. Orr, and Jamond C. Billyard, for their assistance in editing, proofreading, suggestions, and encouragement. I am extremely proud of each one of them.

www.ingramcontent.com/pod-product-compliance
Lightning Source LLC
Chambersburg PA
CBHW071205130626
46555CB00004B/1586